# DENMARK

### FAIRYTALE NORTHERN EUROPE

WHITE STAR PUBLISHERS

*Texts*
Maria Cristina Castellucci

*Photographs*
Marcello Libra

# Contents

1 *The sculpture of the Little Mermaid was created by artist Edvar Eriksen in 1913. The statue, which portrays the leading character from one of Andersen's fairytales, sits on a rock at Kastellet, the fortified district built in the 17th century, and is one of the symbols of Copenhagen.*

2-3 *Ribe, Denmark's oldest city, was founded in the 9th century. The historic district, with its picturesque network of narrow winding streets, looks just like it did hundreds of years ago. The Ribe River was a key communications route for centuries.*

4-5 *Fields stretching as far as the eye can see are one of the distinctive features of the Danish landscape. Despite the fact that the service sector is advancing rapidly, much of the economy is still based on agriculture and breeding.*

6 *Even children participate in the historic reconstructions of the Viking era. These crowded summertime events are popular throughout the country. Parents and children of all ages wear period costumes, taking a trip back in time.*

7 *The Renaissance castle of Egeskov, on Funen Island, was completed in 1554 and has changed very little since then. It was built on a platform of oak trees in the middle of a small lake, and it is the best-preserved moated castle in Northern Europe.*

8-9 *Copenhagen's Nyhavn Canal was transformed in just a few years. It is no longer a disreputable area and has now become one of the capital's trendiest spots. Its picturesque and colorful cottages house some of Copenhagen's most popular cafés and restaurants.*

10-11 *Christmas lights add to the fairytale air of Tivoli Gardens, in the heart of Copenhagen. The trees, fountains and buildings – including the Chinese pagoda, one of the oldest – seem to come alive in the darkness of winter.*

12-13 *The runestones at Jelling are considered among the most significant artifacts left by the Vikings. Engraved on the largest one is the oldest depiction of Christ ever found in Denmark, attesting to the introduction of Christianity into the area by King Harald Bluetooth. This stone is commonly referred to as the "birth certificate" of Denmark because it marks the first time the name of the country was used.*

14-15 *The Viking Ship Museum in Roskilde has five Viking ships that were discovered in the fjord across from the city in 1962. Inaugurated in 1969, it was subsequently enlarged to include a workshop where expert carpenters reconstruct the ships of yore, using ancient models and techniques.*

© 2006 White Star S.p.A.
Via C. Sassone, 22/24
13100 Vercelli, Italy
www.whitestar.it

TRANSLATION
Catherine Bolton

ISBN 88-544-0133-1

*REPRINTS:*
1 2 3 4 5 6    10 09 08 07 06

Printed in Singapore
Color separation: Grafotitoli, Milan

# Introduction

King Harald paused before the master engraver who was carving the last runes on the enormous stone and smiled in satisfaction. He gazed tenderly at the symbols and then turned his eyes to the elegant volutes framing them. They were like the ones adorning the prow and stern of his ship, an intricate and authentic Viking frieze. He slowly circled around to the other side of the boulder, which bore the hieratic image of Christ, arms outstretched and a halo on His head. The king looked across to the wooden chapel he had built between the two grassy mounds nearby, gazing at the northernmost of the two, where his mother and father were buried.

*A job well done*, he thought to himself. A job well done indeed, for the glory of God and of his parents. For a moment, he was overcome with sadness. If his father were still alive, he could have turned to him for advice and asked him what to do in these troubled times. The battles in the long war of conquest, which had continued for decades, seemed endless. And even though things were going well for his people – the Danes had already occupied vast areas of land in both England and France – his new religion, so far removed from ancient beliefs, prevented him from rejoicing fully in this. *A Christian*, he thought. *Who would ever have imagined!* Certainly not his father, who had constantly invoked Odin, the favorite deity of the Danish Vikings and the god of trade, shrewdness and intelligence. Who knows what he would have thought of this monument, of the figure of Christ portrayed here for the very first time? He went back to the other side of the boulder and read the complete inscription: "King Harald ordered this monument erected in memory of his father Gorm and his mother Thyre – the Harald who conquered all of Denmark and Norway, and Christianized the Danes."

Over a thousand years have gone by since that day in AD 960 when Harald Bluetooth completed the enormous runestone honoring his parents. This stone marked a watershed in Danish history because this was the first time the name "Denmark" was used, and the inscription also mentions the introduction of Christianity to the country. As a result, this stone in Jelling, in East Jutland, is commonly referred to as the "birth certificate" of Denmark. It is also significant because it lists the name of Gorm the Old, the first "official" king of Denmark. The Danish royal family descends directly – and uninterruptedly – from this king, making it the oldest monarchy in the world.

Nevertheless, there were other kings before Gorm. In fact, in the 8th century there was a king named Angantyr, in the city of Ribe (South Jutland), and historians also cite King Gudfred, who fought against the Merovingians to maintain control over the territories of Northern Europe, from Frisia to northern Germany.

Though their main interests were trade and agriculture – activities in which they always showed great skill – the Vikings quickly became accustomed to fighting. As a result, we now have the image of a bloodthirsty population devoted to piracy, murder and destruction. In reality, the Vikings who sailed off the coasts of France, England and Ireland and went as far as Greenland, North America and the Mediterranean, were simply seeking new lands to cultivate. A Viking fleet besieged Paris in 880, demanding an exorbitant amount of money as well as land on which to settle; in exchange, the Vikings would leave the city in peace. As a result, some of the Norsemen were given fiefdoms on the coast. One of these came to be known as Normandy, and various historical events would soon link this area with southern Italy and Sicily. But that is another story.

Let's get back to Denmark, the country from which the Vikings set sail in their splendid wooden ships. Their ancient culture has left countless signs here, from fortifications to necropolises, and the country's museums display numerous artifacts from this period, like the five Viking ships from the 11th century now at Roskilde.

Naturally, the Vikings were not the first population to live in Denmark. Before the tribe of the Danes had migrated here from Sweden in AD 500, groups of nomadic hunters had already shared this territory for millennia. Thousands of dolmens bear witness to the populations of the Stone Age, and hundreds of tumuli have yielded objects that paint a picture of a primitive culture that was nevertheless created somewhat refined works. Naturally, however, these artifacts were nothing like the ones produced during the Bronze Age. For example, the Chariot of the Sun (*Solvognen*), discovered in Sjælland (Zealand) in 1902 and displayed at the National Museum in Copenhagen, is an extraordinary work made of bronze and gold and revealing rather advanced craftsmanship.

Like many other objects – horns, helmets, hatchets and so on – the chariot was discovered in a peat bog, a typical environment in which to find Danish artifacts and yielding many surprises for archaeologists. The most extraordinary finding was the Tollund Man, who was hanged in the 2nd century BC (Iron Age) and thrown into a bog, where his body was preserved virtually intact until 1950 (his head and a copy of his body are displayed at the Silkeborg Museum). But there is also the Grauballe Man, who was about 30 years old when he died. His intact body was discovered in a peat bog over 2,000 years later (his body is now at the Moesgaard Museum near Århus). Countless other items have also been discovered, some of which are quite valuable, such as the golden horns from Gallehus (they were stolen in 1802 and melted down to make other objects – a set of gold earrings were found recently that have been traced to the gold from these horns).

The Danes love their history. The country is dotted with museums with exhibitions about ancient times as well as Denmark's more recent farming culture. They are often "living" museums: actors are often used to create faithful reproductions of different eras, and visitors are often allowed to touch the artifacts, don costumes and participate in exhibitions.

For example, there are museums that faithfully reconstruct old Danish cities (in Odense, Copenhagen and Århus), with people dressed in 18- and 19th-century costumes who perform the daily tasks of yesteryear. This is what has been done at the Lejre Experimental Centre (*Lejre forsøgcenter*) of history and archaeology, where an Iron Age settlement has been reconstructed based on meticulous scientific criteria. There is a long waiting list of families that want to embark on a journey back in time by dressing and acting just like their ancestors did thousands of years ago. Another example is the National Museum in Copenhagen, which has special rooms where children can dress like Vikings and play with ships and castles.

This list could go on and includes Viking villages, science museums and aquariums, where visitors can even touch the fish, and countless annual historical festivals and commemorations. For the Danes, culture is not a sterile separate entity or something remote and intangible; it is an experience for everyone. This is also emblematic of the instinctive friendliness that is probably the most evident trait of these people, together with their conviviality. One of the most important elements in Danish life is the concept of *hygge*. This completely untranslatable term essentially means the pleasure of spending time together – for a cup of coffee, a walk on the beach or in the woods, a chat or to listen to some good music. In many ways, it is what inspires the Danes' passion for festivities. Any occasion is perfect for getting together and celebrating for hours on end: birthdays, company parties and especially Christmas, which is "serious business" here and is organized weeks in advance. Houses are decorated with evergreen wreaths, garlands and *nisser* (the little gnomes of popular tradition) made of a variety of materials. Cakes and cookies are prepared according to traditional recipes. On the four Sundays before Christmas, families get together for Advent and light the candles – one by one – on the traditional Advent wreath, drink *gløgg* (wine flavored with ginger, cinnamon and cloves) and sing Christmas carols.

Singing is also a distinctively Danish tradition and to outsiders it might seem that the Danes do nothing but sing: on the first day of school (however, years ago children sang every morning), at every commemoration and even at funerals. For birthdays, weddings, baptisms and other celebrations, songs are composed especially for the guest of honor and all the other guests join in to sing.

The ancient Dannebrog, the Danish flag, is also present at every Danish event. No house is without a pennant that is displayed for public and private celebrations alike, and little paper flags make their festive appearance on birthday cakes, on Christmas trees, in shop windows and on anything else that can possibly be decorated.

Indeed, the Danes are inordinately proud of their flag, which is the oldest one in the world and boasts supernatural origins. According to legend, the flag fell from heaven during the victorious battle led by King Valdemar in Estonia in 1219, an event to which – naturally – a special celebration is dedicated.

*16 top  With nearly 700 graves, Lindholm Høje is one of the largest Viking burial sites. Stones were placed around the graves in an oval to evoke the shape of a ship. Rulers and important figures were often buried inside real boats.*

*16 bottom  The Danes are passionate about their history and celebrate their Viking roots with special events. Most of them take place in different locations during the summer and include historic commemorations, theme markets and processions in period costumes.*

*17  At outdoor museums, costumed figures recreate the atmosphere of times past and perform the daily activities of their ancestors. Visitors are often allowed to participate, making this a true journey back in time.*

In effect, however, this auspicious episode was merely a happy interlude in a reign that weakened gradually between the end of the Viking era and the 14th century. Fortune did not smile again on Denmark until Margaret I ascended to the throne (1387-1412) and united Denmark, Sweden and Norway into a single kingdom (Denmark and Norway were ruled under the Danish crown until 1814). The queen – and most of the Danish monarchs – are buried in the great cathedral of Roskilde, which was built in about the year 1000. This city became important when Harald Bluetooth left Jelling in about 980 to transfer his residence here, building a wooden church in which he was later buried. Roskilde subsequently became the center of Episcopal power, which vied with royal power. The city was also the home of Absalon, the bishop who founded not only the cathedral, which still stands, but also the city of Copenhagen.

Visiting the cathedral, which UNESCO has inscribed on the World Heritage List, is like taking a walk through a history book, with the monarchs' tombs marking each chapter. One of these kings was Christian IV, who ruled the country from 1588 to 1648 and is now remembered above all for his influence on architecture. He built the fairytale castle of Rosenborg, the Round Tower (*Rundetårn*), the building that housed the old Stock Exchange (*Børsen*) in Copenhagen, and the stately Frederiksborg Castle at Hillerød, which is often called the "Danish Versailles."

Nevertheless, Christian IV, who became known as the Architect King, was neither the first nor the last monarch to devote himself to building. Between 1574 and 1585, his father Frederick II ordered the construction of what is probably Denmark's most famous castle: Kronborg. Built over a 15th-century fortress overlooking the Strait of Øresund near the city of Helsingør, it owes its fame to Shakespeare, who used it as the setting for the tragic tale of Hamlet. The statue of national hero Holger Danske is safeguarded in the castle dungeon. Asleep with his sword and shield at his side, this powerful warrior will reawaken if Denmark is ever in grave danger.

In effect, however, Holger Danske has already had several occasions to rouse from his slumber. Between 1658 and 1660, Denmark was about to surrender to Sweden and only the desperate defense of the capital averted annexation. In 1807 the English fleet bombarded Copenhagen, which had allied itself with Napoleon. The country was forced to surrender. This dealt the final blow to an already shaky economy, and the Danish government finally declared bankruptcy in 1813. This situation was a far cry from the times when the Danes and their fleet controlled trade across the northern seas and their king claimed sovereignty over an immense territory stretching from Central America to Iceland. Norway gained its independence the following year – 1814. In 1917 the colonies in the Antilles were sold to the United States, and in 1944 Iceland also declared its independence.

20-21 *As soon as the sun comes out, restaurants and cafés move their tables outside, and at the busiest times of the day it is practically impossible to find a seat. The Danes are very sociable – and they are also big coffee drinkers. Any occasion is a good chance to enjoy a cup of coffee with friends.*

20 bottom left *In all Danish cities, bicycles are the preferred means of transportation for people of all ages. There are bike paths along all the main roads, from the capital to the smallest towns.*

20 bottom right *Even in Denmark's larger cities, parks are home to countless animals, including deer, which are so accustomed to people that they do not shy away from them.*

breeding are the most important economic sectors, closely followed by the service sector.

Though they hail from a very small country, the Danes are extremely proud of their past, as well as their individuality and uniqueness. In the 20th century, the country established an enviable social-welfare system that covers citizens from birth to death, and the Danes naturally defend it with every possible means. Though the country has joined the European Union, the Danes tend to keep their distance from it, grasping every opportunity to underscore their independence. As a result, the Euro was not introduced into the country, as the common currency was rejected in 2000 by a national referendum.

The educational system is also an enormous source of pride and is based on the ideas of bishop-poet Nikolai F. S. Grundtvig and educator Christen Kold. In the mid-19th century, the two established free schools for the population (*folkeskoler*). Even today, these schools – together with the countless libraries in every town – practice what is known as "permanent education." This is one of the reasons that the Danes generally have a high level of education and are distinguished by their civic-mindedness, instilled in them from early childhood. Respect for oneself and others also extends to respect for nature and the environment, a sector in which the Danes are decidedly at the cutting edge. They have also achieved this through the use of alternative sources of energy, restrictions to protect the environment, the widespread habit of recycling raw materials and other environmental initiatives. In fact, despite the Atlantic climate, with frosty winters, cool summers and plenty of rainfall, the Danes love outdoor living. It is not unusual to see people out for a stroll in the pouring rain or freezing cold – even on the beach. As soon as the mercury starts to rise, parks fill up and waiters bring their café tables outside, ready to provide their patrons with blankets if necessary.

This is why vacation homes – often just simple wooden cottages – are in great demand, despite the fact that most of the population lives in urban areas (though only the capital can actually be considered a "big city," with a population of 500,000 that virtually triples if the entire metropolitan area is included). In fact, the single-family house with a garden, the model that characterizes the suburbs of Denmark's biggest cities, is still the Danish ideal. Those who can't afford one settle for a *kolonihave*, a small plot of land that is part of a common garden and holds a little wooden cabin, which is a sought-after weekend retreat.

In short, the Danes enjoy a very relaxed lifestyle that is reflected in every aspect of social life: no formality – as demonstrated by the fact that even the formal "you" form (*De*) has virtually been abolished – coupled with very little bureaucracy, an utterly practical approach to all matters and trust in others. All this has contributed enormously to the modernization and "deprovincialization" of Danish society, a process that has gained great momentum over the past decade.

In short, by the end of World War II Denmark had acquired its current geopolitical features. It is a small country with an area of about 16,600 square miles of plains, forests and lakes. It occupies the peninsula of Jutland and 500 islets and islands, the largest of which is Sjælland, the site of Copenhagen, the capital city. From an administrative standpoint, Greenland, the world's largest island, and the archipelago of Fær Øer (Faroe), a group of about 20 islands and reefs dotting the sea between Scotland and Iceland, also belong to Denmark. However, both of these territories enjoy great autonomy. Denmark is a constitutional monarchy that is currently ruled by the beloved Queen Margaret II, who has been on the throne since 1972. It has a population of approximately 5.2 million people, nearly half of whom live in the four main cities: Copenhagen, the capital; Århus and Aalborg, respectively in central and northern Jutland; Odense, on the Funen Island. Agriculture and

Copenhagen has recently come to the forefront as the liveliest and most vibrant of the northern capitals; this is demonstrated not only by the growing influx of tourists, but also by increased foreign investments, the number of new buildings and infrastructures that have been constructed recently and the redevelopment of entire districts. All tours of the city revolve around the monuments of the past, like Christiansborg Castle, where Bishop Absalon built the first fortress (the castle now houses the Danish Parliament), the Church of Our Lady (*Vor Frue Kirke*) with exquisite statues by sculptor Bertel Thorvaldsen, the Church of Our Savior (*Vor Frelsers Kirke*), with its soaring spire that can be accessed via a daring staircase, the stately Marble Church (*Marmorkirken*), located across from the sprawling complex of Amalienborg Palace (the queen's residence), and many other breathtaking edifices built at Christian IV's behest. Nevertheless, Copenhagen's architecture has now been enriched with contemporary works. The Royal Library – nicknamed "The Black Diamond" – and the new Opera House are just two of the most recent examples of the "building craze" that has recently pervaded Denmark, culminating with the construction of the futuristic Øresund

Bridge linking Denmark and Sweden. Yet Copenhagen has remained a city "on a human scale" where people still get around mainly on bicycles. It is a place with extensive green areas, like the parks of Kongens Have and Frederiksberg, the Tivoli amusement park that has been in the heart of town for over 150 years, the enormous pedestrian area of Strøget, which starts at the broad Rådhuspladsen, or City Hall Square, charming plazas like Gråbrødretorv, Amagertorv and Kongens Nytorv and rows of shops, cafés and restaurants. Even the military area of Kastellet has been cleared of its naval trappings and converted into an area where people can enjoy a relaxing stroll or sunbathe on the lawns. From here, they can take in the seaside vista and watch cruise ships as they dock in the very heart of the city, virtually around the corner from the royal palace of Amalienborg, where the port area has undergone extensive redevelopment. Of course, no tour would be complete without stopping to see the Little Mermaid (*Lille Havfrue*), the symbol of the city. This little statue, perched on a rock at the end of the Langelinie seafront, attracts flocks of tourists every day. Made in 1913, the sculpture is merely the most famous of all the expressions of a veritable cult that has arisen around Hans Christian Andersen.

The famous writer, known above all for his fairytales, was also the author of novels, travel books and lyric poetry; a museum dedicated to him has been built next to the house where he grew up, in the city of Odense. The museum features collections of books, manuscripts, photographs and objects that belonged to Andersen, displayed in a modern multimedia setting. The museum is surrounded by half-timbered houses and paved streets that, to some extent, have preserved the appearance of the town as it was during Andersen's lifetime. Ribe, in south Jutland, is the oldest city in Denmark (8th century) and it has maintained a charming and

picturesque ambience. Virtually the entire historic district is protected by extremely strict conservation measures, and there is a splendid Romanesque cathedral in the center. Once a Viking city, for centuries it was an important trade center along the routes connecting the Baltic to the coasts of Northern Europe. A stroll through Ribe's narrow, winding streets is like stepping back in time. In fact, 100 of Ribe's buildings are considered national monuments and have fully maintained their mediaeval appearance.

One of Denmark's most interesting natural environments is located just a few miles west of Ribe. This is Vadehavet, or the Wadden Sea, an enormous

*22-23 The Gefion Fountain in Copenhagen is named after the goddess of fertility who, according to legend, asked King Gylfe for a homeland. He told her that she could take as much land in Sweden as she could plow in one night. The goddess turned her sons into oxen and managed to plow the area now known as Sjælland.*

*23 The Tivoli amusement park is located in the heart of Copenhagen, and it has been one of the city's favorite attractions for over 150 years. Children's rides, beautifully manicured gardens, light shows, fabulous entertainment in the auditorium and around the park, restaurants and fountains make Tivoli a magical place.*

lagoon lined with seemingly endless beaches. In fact, the entire west coast of Denmark is a stunning spectacle of nature, with long sandy beaches edged by sand dunes that are continuously carved and reshaped by the wind. Beyond the sand there are moors dotted with low-growing heather, and woods inhabited by small mammals and dozens of bird species.

This is a harsh, wild environment that is exposed to the inclement weather of the Atlantic, but this is precisely what makes it so fascinating and striking. It is also distinguished by its unusual light, which has inspired countless artists. In the late 19th century, for example, an artists' colony was established at Skagen, at the northern end of the Jutland peninsula where the land narrows into a sandy tongue and two seas meet. The artists' works, which are displayed at the local museum – but also at leading Danish and Scandinavian galleries – celebrate wild, resplendent nature.

The same concept has essentially been followed in recent years by designing and building art museums in areas with stunning vistas. The most recent is the Arken Museum of Modern Art, which rests like a ship along the shore a few miles south of Copenhagen, but there are also others, like the North Jutland Museum of Art (*Nordjyllands Kunstmuseum*) in Aalborg, which was designed by Alvar Aalto in the late Sixties, and the Louisiana, the most important Danish modern art museum, which overlooks the Strait of Øresund.

Not far from the Louisiana, there is another museum-house in an equally dramatic setting. This one is dedicated to Karen Blixen, one of the best-known and most widely translated Danish writers in the world. It still has the original furnishings from the period in which the famous author of *Out of Africa* and *Seven Gothic Tales* lived here (she died in 1962 and is buried on the grounds).

A brief look at the list of famous Danes – in addition to Andersen and Blixen, we can also cite philosopher Søren Kierkegaard, Niels Bohr, who was awarded the Nobel Prize in Physics, film directors Carl T. Dreyer and Lars von Trier, and sculptor Bertel Thorvaldsen – immediately makes it evident that Danish artists and scientists have always strived for excellence and worldwide success. This is exactly what happened a few years ago with Peter Høeg, whose book *Smilla's Sense of Snow* became an international bestseller. They are not the only notables from Denmark, however, as demonstrated by Lego, which has exported millions of multicolored blocks for decades – to the delight of generations of children around the world.

In general, Danish design has garnered great success thanks to its appealing combination of imagination and practicality. There are plenty of examples, like Arne Jacobsen's Ant Chair and Egg Chair, the sophisticated silver items by Georg Jensen, stereos and modern television sets by Bang & Olufsen, Royal Copenhagen china, Holmegaard glass and the soft and elegant furs designed by Birger Christensen.

*24 top  Ribe, founded by the Vikings, is now a charming maze of narrow streets. This is the perfect place for a leisurely stroll to discover the town's past as an important trade center.*

*24 bottom  The house where Hans Christian Andersen was born, in Odense, has tiny rooms with wooden floors and beamed ceilings. A modern multimedia museum has been annexed to the old building and offers a wealth of information to those who want to learn more about this extraordinary writer.*

*24-25  Half-timbered houses are still very common in urban historic districts as well as rural areas. The oldest ones – like this one at Nedergade, in Odense, which houses an original old-fashioned emporium – are meticulously restored and protected.*

Hundreds of craftsmen, who have transformed their trade into an art, have followed in the wake of these famous designers. Ceramics, candles, soft knitwear, shawls, glassware, household items, pillows and jewelry are distinguished by the very highest quality – but with that touch of "Danishness" that adds to their charm. One of the spots with the highest concentration of workshops and studios is Bornholm Island, in the Baltic. Set at the easternmost edge of Denmark, it is the adopted home of painters, sculptors and numerous craftsmen who have found inspiration here for their creations. As opposed to the rest of Denmark, which has a rather flat or rolling countryside, the island is rocky, with steep, jagged cliffs along its coastlines. Its stunning natural environment, unusually mild climate, delightful villages, round church-fortresses – unique in Denmark – and the spectacular ruins of the great 13th-century fortress of Hammershus have made it a favorite tourist destination. The island is also famous for its culinary delights. The smokehouses dotting its shores offer traditional smoked herring, a seafood specialty expertly prepared by the people of Bornholm.

This is one of those classic dishes that people either love or hate, a characteristic shared by many traditional dishes here. Danish cuisine is quite different from what most foreigners are accustomed to eating, especially visitors from the Mediterranean. For example, there is *smørrebrød*, a typical open sandwich made of rye bread and served with pickled herring or pork-liver pâté and other delicacies, and washed down with a glass of *snaps* (aquavit). *Øllebrød*, a sweet soup, is another traditional dish. However, Danish cuisine is also being modernized now. The reinterpretation of dishes by creative young chefs has earned many restaurants a place in the Michelin Guide, as well as appreciation from the public.

Nevertheless, everyone agrees on two specialties: sweets and, above all, beer. The national beverage has been produced since ancient times, and even the popular legends about elves and trolls are full of characters busily stirring steaming cauldrons of beer. The first royal brewery dates back to 1454, but today the market is dominated by Carlsberg and Tuborg, which produce many varieties of this aromatic brew. The Danes are proud of their beer, which is best enjoyed directly from the classic green bottle (the *bajer*) any time of the day. Though it is no longer customary to drink it at breakfast, beer is served at both lunch and dinner, during work breaks and at parties. It is an excuse to stop for a chat, naturally to discuss the weather – characteristically changeable – and taxes, ever a source of complaint, though probably more out of habit than anything else. Because the Danes are absolutely confident about one thing: it's not Denmark that's small, but the rest of the world that's big. And Denmark is in the very heart of it all.

*26-27 Round churches – the one in the photograph, located in Østerlars, is dedicated to St. Lawrence and was built in the 11th century – are one of the unique features of Bornholm Island. Their distinctive shape is evident even at a distance.*

*27 bottom left The monumental entrance to the Carlsberg brewery was built in the second half of the 19th century, alongside other eclectic structures. The brewery is one of the largest in the world and is open to visitors. The tour naturally includes a tasting session!*

*27 bottom right Beer is unquestionably the national drink of Denmark. The Vikings drank it and the first "official" brewery dates back to the 16th century. It comes in a number of varieties, and there is even a special Christmas beer known as juleøl.*

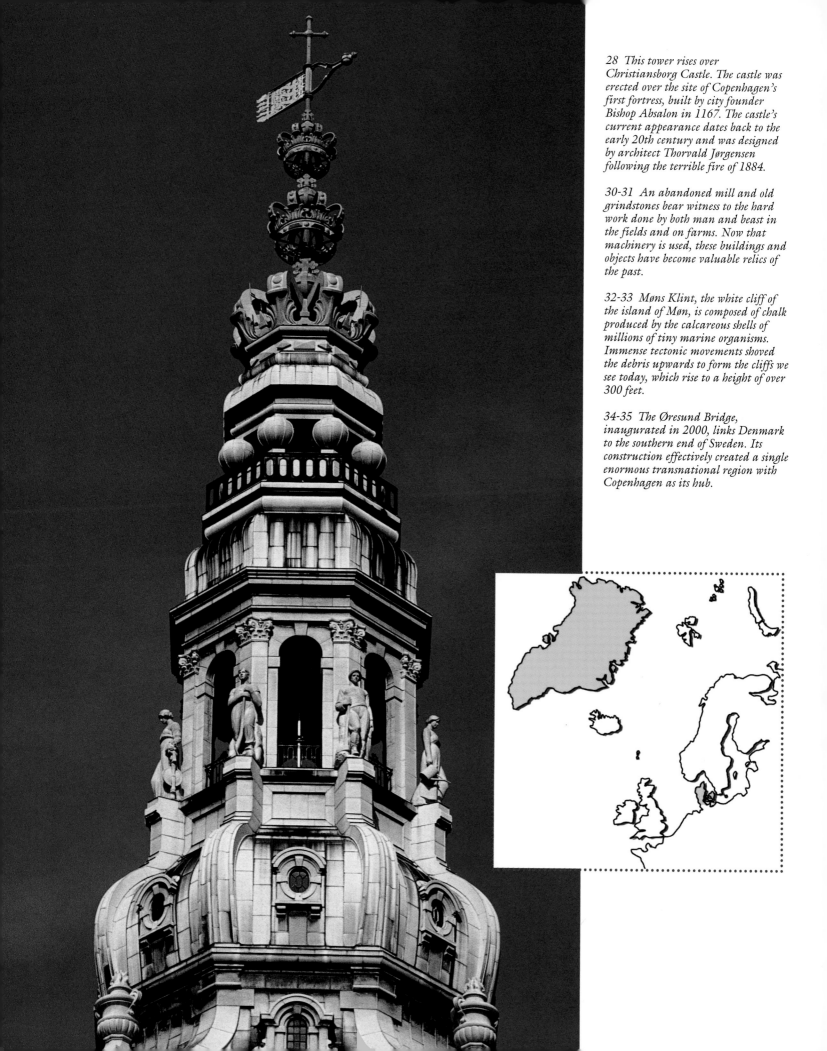

**28** This tower rises over Christiansborg Castle. The castle was erected over the site of Copenhagen's first fortress, built by city founder Bishop Absalon in 1167. The castle's current appearance dates back to the early 20th century and was designed by architect Thorvald Jørgensen following the terrible fire of 1884.

**30-31** An abandoned mill and old grindstones bear witness to the hard work done by both man and beast in the fields and on farms. Now that machinery is used, these buildings and objects have become valuable relics of the past.

**32-33** Møns Klint, the white cliff of the island of Møn, is composed of chalk produced by the calcareous shells of millions of tiny marine organisms. Immense tectonic movements shoved the debris upwards to form the cliffs we see today, which rise to a height of over 300 feet.

**34-35** The Øresund Bridge, inaugurated in 2000, links Denmark to the southern end of Sweden. Its construction effectively created a single enormous transnational region with Copenhagen as its hub.

# The charm of the lowlands

*36 top Svaneke is Denmark's smallest and easternmost port.
The activities that once made it a thriving town have now been replaced almost entirely by businesses catering to the tourist trade.*

*36 bottom Ripe ears of wheat are ready to be harvested. In the soft summer breeze, the fields are transformed into a rippling sea of gold under the sapphire sky. These rural landscapes represent some of Denmark's most striking scenery.*

*37 The old mills have now been abandoned, replaced by more modern systems. Nevertheless, these structures are still very common in Denmark's rural areas, and many have now been restored as homes.*

# Skagen, towards Scandinavia

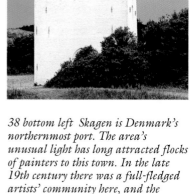

*38 top left  The drifting sand dune of Råbjerg Mile is one of Denmark's most intriguing natural phenomena. The dune, which is about 130 feet high and over half a mile long, shifts eastward by about 26 feet a year, covering everything in its path and continuously transforming the landscape.*

*38 center left  A wind rose marks the directions at Grenen, the far end of the Danish peninsula, where the waves of two seas (Skagerrak to the west and Kattegat to the east) create strong currents. The sandy beach is so narrow that you can stand with one foot in each sea.*

*38 bottom left  Skagen is Denmark's northernmost port. The area's unusual light has long attracted flocks of painters to this town. In the late 19th century there was a full-fledged artists' community here, and the Skagen Museum has an excellent collection of their works.*

*38 right and 38-39  Over the years the moving sands, incessantly shifted by the wind, have covered parts of many structures and, in some cases, have swallowed up entire buildings. The Buried Church (Den Tilsandede Kirke) is actually just the bell tower of the old church of Skagen, and most of the Råbjerg Knude Lighthouse (right) is also covered.*

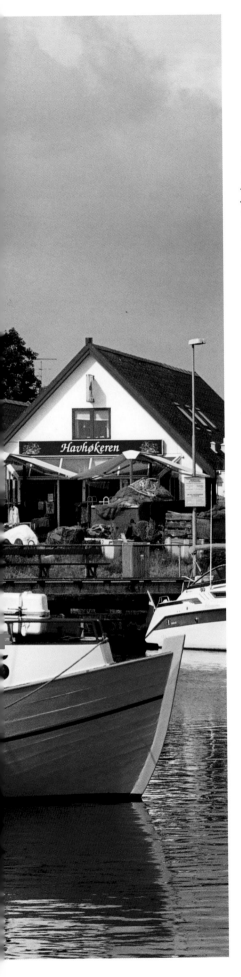

40-41 and 41 Thousands of miles of coastline were an irresistible attraction for the Vikings, but also for fishermen – even now. Because of its geography, with countless islands and a very long coastline, Denmark boasts an ancient tradition of deep-sea and inshore fishing. In fact, fish is a basic ingredient in many traditional Danish dishes. Some areas of the country still have old smokehouses, where fish is smoked and cooked the old-fashioned way. However, fishing did not develop into an important economic activity until the late 19th century, when it became easier to transport the product. Herring is the most common fish in the seas of Denmark, and it is eaten fresh or preserved (marinated herring is a favorite, served with schnapps or Danish aquavit). Cod and plaice are also plentiful. Most fishermen work independently or are part of cooperatives, with medium-sized fishing boats that crisscross the Baltic and North Seas just like those of their ancestors did. When they are not at sea, the vessels rock lazily in Skagen harbor, creating a picturesque scene of swaying masts. The fishermen, aboard ship or on the docks, prepare for the next outing, as seen in these pictures from the port of Skagen.

# Wind-whipped landscapes

*42-43, 43 and 44-45 Jutland, the peninsular region of Denmark, is the country's main agricultural area, with sweeping flat landscapes and cultivated fields. It is a palette of greens, browns and yellows dotted with flowers, whose presence testifies to the gradual abandonment of pesticides in favor of agricultural methods that respect man and nature. Barley, wheat, rye and oats, which ripen and harvest at different times, enormous beet and potato fields and orchards create enchanting interplays of color. Between the fields and extensive grazing lands – Denmark has about 10 million pigs, double its human population, and a little over 2.5 million head of cattle – there are farms and small villages, giving the landscape its distinctive appearance. The countryside is also dotted with woods and forests, heaths, marshes, peat bogs and protected areas. Although the contribution of agriculture and animal breeding to the economy has diminished significantly over the past 50 years, they are still fundamental, as they provide most of the raw material for the food industry, one of the most profitable sectors in the Danish economy.*

*46  Golden wheat, blue skies dotted with white clouds, a simple country bell tower off in the distance and dark green copses: the Danish countryside offers visitors the pure lines of a romantic painting.*

47  *With their neatly tended fields, trees lining the cultivated areas and a kaleidoscope of colors – cool, soothing greens and soft, warm yellows – the farmlands have an inherent simplicity that conveys sheer beauty but also a sense of freedom and open space.*

48 top and 48-49 Sjælland is
Denmark's largest and most
important island. This is where the
capital and its vast metropolitan area
are located, but the island also boasts
a marvelous and varied natural
environment. Turbines, used to
harness wind power, are a frequent
sight amidst the fields. One-fifth of
Denmark's electrical energy comes
from wind power, and, in terms of
percentage, it is the European leader
in this sector. Here again, modernity
goes hand in hand with
environmental concerns.

48 center and bottom  The Lake
District near the town of Silkeborg, in
central Jutland, is a very picturesque
area. Lakes and woods alternate in
this rolling countryside. In the
summer, the lakes and rivers can be
explored in period boats, the oldest of
which was built in 1861. This area
has the country's tallest landforms,
which are actually low hills. They only
look big in relation to the rest of the
area: the tallest rises to a height of just
577 feet above sea level.

50-51  Windmills are generally considered a symbol of Holland, but the Danish countryside also has many (the ones here are in northern Jutland). Once the hub of arduous farming activities, windmills have now become picturesque vestiges of the past that are carefully protected because of their beauty and historic value.

51 top  Golf is one of Denmark's favorite pastimes. The country's unique geographic layout – prevalently flat but with broad hilly areas – is ideal for golf courses. In Scandinavia golfing is no longer an exclusive sport: though the clubs have maintained their traditional style, they are open to everyone.

51 center and bottom  The play of light and color is at its best in the summer. Golden fields rippling in the wind, forests, roofs made of red tiles or dark slate, lush fields of wildflowers and lakes seem to be the work of a masterly painter enthralled by the contrasting colors and gentle lines of nature.

51

# The northern islands

*52-53 and 53 top  Møns Klint is the name of another tall and beautiful chalky white cliff along the east side of Møn Island, south of Copenhagen. The cliff, about 5 miles long and nearly 330 feet high, is composed of fine chalk – just like the kind we use to write on blackboards. The beech-crowned summit of Møns Klint has wide hiking trails through the woods, and belvederes afford stunning views of the extraordinary turquoise sea and the steep cliffs. A set of over 150 steps leads to the bottom of the cliff, where there is a long rocky beach with countless sea fossils, particularly cuttlefish and sea urchins.*

*53 center and bottom  The rural landscape of the Møn Island closely resembles the countryside of nearby Sjælland. Here too, the polychrome patchwork of fields stretches as far as the eye can see, extending to the coastline. Some of the island farmers have formed a consortium that publishes an annual guide about where to purchase organic and high-quality products.*

54-55 and 55 top  The port of Klintholm is on the southern coast of Møn Island. It was originally established as a fishing village, and even today fishing is widely practiced. More and more, however, yachts are moored alongside fishing boats, as tourism has also become an important part of the local economy.

55 center  Antoine Gerad de La Calmette built the little castle of Liselund for his wife Lise in the late 18th century. It is at Møns Klint, in the middle of a romantic park that the owners designed based on Rousseau's theories. The castle, a low building with a thatched roof, is reflected in a small lake dotted with water lilies.

55 bottom  The charming 13th-century church of Fanefjord Kirke is about 8 miles from Stege, the capital of Møn Island. The interior has lovely 16th-century frescoes done in the Nordic style.

56-57  Møn Island boasts splendid bucolic landscapes. As you sit in the shade of a leafy tree, gazing across the endless expanse of wheat fields and breathing the clean country air, you can't help but feel at peace with the world.

# Ærø, the mariners' route

*58 top left Skjoldnæs Lighthouse, on Ærø Island, has guided sailors for centuries. This island is part of the South Funen archipelago, a popular attraction for pleasure boaters that is always crowded in the summer. There are 90 islands, large and small, but only 25 of them are inhabited. Some are connected to Funen Island by bridges, whereas others can be reached only by ferry.*

*58 top right, center and bottom Ærø Island has two separate municipal administrations that work together on the ambitious project of making the island self-sufficient in terms of power by exploiting renewable energy such as wind and solar power. This strong environmental commitment has helped make the island's countryside one of the most beautiful and well kept, with orderly rows of grain fields. The landscape is dotted with carefully restored old buildings such as windmills and low farmhouses with thatched roofs. For the residents of this island, one of the few that is not linked by a modern bridge but still relies on ferries, maintaining the environment is a point of honor.*

*58-59 This aerial view shows the unusual shape of Ærø Island, which looks like a raft extending into the sea. Its little houses seem to huddle together in the immense green fields.*

60-61 and 61  The town of
Ærøskøbing is the capital and main
port of Ærø Island. Here, time
magically seems to have stopped in the
18th century. From its half-timbered
houses and its Renaissance- and
Empire-style homes, dozens of which
are protected by strict laws (36 have
been declared national monuments),
to its narrow cobblestone streets that
open onto charming little squares, the
carved and brightly painted doors
framed by climbing roses and
hollyhocks, the little windows with lace
curtains and porcelain knick-knacks
on the windowsills and the old 17th-
century market, which is still
beautifully preserved, everything here
conveys a sense of romance.
This idyllic setting, carefully preserved
by the townspeople, gives the 21st-
century traveler a perfect idea of what
a Danish fishing and trade village
must have looked like in the 17th and
18th centuries. In the small city
museum, period furnishings and
objects reconstruct the original rooms,
for a true journey back in time.

62-63 Unlike the rest of Denmark, Bornholm Island is rocky. The inlets, formed where the mountains meet the sea, paint an enchanting picture. For miles and miles, nature reigns supreme: there are only a few fishermen here and not a single boat is seen on the horizon.

63 top The white sand of Dueodde is so fine that it was used to fill hourglasses. The beach is popular with bathers, attracted by the clear water around the island and the beautiful sandy shores.

63 center The fortress of Hammershus was built in the heart of the enormous protected area of Nordbornholm during the 13th century and was once both a fortress and a residence. Only a few portions of the outside walls and three towers are still standing.

# Bornholm, in the heart of the Baltic

*63 bottom  The picturesque town of Gudhjem overlooks the Baltic. Its small harbor is popular among boaters, particularly in the summer, when unpredictably warm northern breezes make for perfect sailing weather.*

64-65 *Round churches are found only at Bornholm. They were built in the late Middle Ages and were originally used as fortresses to protect residents against the marauding pirates who infested the Baltic. This explains their thick walls and the fact that they have very few openings. The main one is at Østerlars (in the picture). It is three stories tall, and the gallery once used by archers is still visible.*

65 *top and center left The church at Nylars (top) is not as old as the others but is the best preserved. The church at Nyker (center left) is the smallest and is just two stories tall. Like the church of Østerlars, its interior is decorated with 14th-century frescoes of the Passion.*

65 *center right The distinctive architecture of Bornholm's smokehouses, with enormous square chimneypots, can be seen in various towns along the coast. The fishing and smoking industries – chiefly for herring – now largely cater to the tourist trade. The smokehouses have little restaurants where visitors can try fish dishes prepared according to island recipes.*

65 *bottom Bornholm is the largest and easternmost of the Danish islands. Its residents have always been attentive to environmental concerns, alternative energy sources and recycling. As a result, it is dotted with tall structures used to generate wind power.*

# The future behind ancient walls

66 top  The Town Hall of Odense, which overlooks a large square at the edge of the city's pedestrian area, was built in 1883 in an eclectic style that blends elements inspired by Italian Renaissance architecture with Neo-Gothic forms to create a charming building.

66 bottom  Ribe is one of the oldest towns in Denmark. Over 100 buildings in its historic district are national monuments and have maintained their mediaeval appearance.

67  The distinctive features of Hans Christian Andersen, one of Denmark's most famous figures and unquestionably the most famous internationally, are captured by the bronze statue next to City Hall in Copenhagen, the writer's adopted city.

*68-69  Copenhagen's City Hall was inaugurated in 1905. Built in an eclectic style, it blends Italian Renaissance elements with references to the citadels of the Middle Ages. Six statues of sentinels in Renaissance garb stand guard along the top of the façade.*

# Copenhagen and its environs

69 top  The bronze group portraying the Lurblæserne, or "Lur" players, is set on a tall, thick column in City Hall Square. The Lur was an ancient spiral horn documented by archaeological findings dating to the 2nd to 1st centuries BC. The sculpture was cast by Sigfried Wagner in 1914.

69 center and bottom  City Hall Square is the lively heart of Copenhagen. Two of the city's main roads feed into the square. City Hall Square is always crowded because it also marks the beginning of the pedestrian mall that leads to nearby Tivoli Gardens. It is a popular rendezvous – day and night – to tour the city, go shopping or visit museums.

70-71 and 71 center left  Strøget, the city's pedestrian route, is over a mile long and is the main street in the historic district. Lined with all kinds of shops and rows of elegant old buildings, it was the world's first pedestrian mall.

71 top left  The Stork Fountain (Storkespringvandet) in the middle of Amagertorv Square was built in the 19th century.

71 top right  The Round Tower (Rundetårn) was built by King Christian IV from 1637 to 1642 together with other buildings as part of a Renaissance complex. It was used as a base for the university astronomical observatory.

71 center right  The Church of Our Lady (Vor Frue Kirke) is Copenhagen's Lutheran cathedral. Though it is the city's oldest, it was reconstructed in a Neoclassical style in the early 19th century after it was bombed. The imposing statues of the apostles that line the brightly lit nave are the work of sculptor Bertel Thorvaldsen.

71 bottom  Viewed from the air, Copenhagen is a delightful mix of ancient and modern buildings, with tiled roofs and bell towers set alongside more recent structures. City zoning regulations have long banned the construction of particularly tall buildings in order to preserve Copenhagen's skyline.

72 top  Canals, most of which are artificial, run alongside carriageways, testifying to an era in which access to the sea was fundamental for facilitating trade. In fact, the name of the capital comes from the Old Danish word *Köppmannæhafn*, meaning "Merchants, Port"

72 center  A stroll through the city reveals the Danes' passion for sculpture. Celebratory statues – like the equestrian statues of the founder of Copenhagen, Bishop Absalon (left), and of King Frederick VII (right) – can be seen alongside works by contemporary artists (center).

72 bottom  The Black Diamond, the extension of Copenhagen's Royal Library, was inaugurated in 1999. Its modern architecture, which surprisingly fits in with the old buildings in the area, evokes the shape of a treasure chest, alluding to the wealth of knowledge inside.

72-73  The Stock Exchange was built from 1619 to 1940 by Christian IV, who was also known as the Architect King. At one end there is an intriguing spire, formed by the long tails of four dragons and supposedly designed by the king himself.

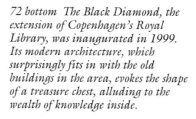

74

74-75 and 75 *The Christmas season is one of the prettiest times to visit Denmark and Copenhagen. Christmas has always been one of the Danes' favorite holidays. By mid-November – or the first Sunday of Advent at the very latest – every house is gaily decorated for the season. Most of the decorations are made by hand, and families get together before the holiday season to work on them together. A stroll through town clearly reveals the Danes' passion for Christmas decorations: streets and buildings are bedecked in an extravaganza of lights, garlands, Christmas trees, hearts, stars and countless other motifs.*
*This is a feast for the eyes and heart, especially when evening falls – in*

*winter it is dark by four o'clock – and all the lights turn on, transforming the city into a kaleidoscope of color. The Christmas markets are a must, particularly the one open at Tivoli until December 23rd. They are the perfect places to find handmade decorations, candles for the tree (real candles are used in Denmark and throughout Scandinavia), braided paper hearts and paper baskets to fill with sweets and hang on the branches. Naturally, there are stalls that serve mulled wine, flavored with cinnamon and ginger (gløgg), and apple doughnuts (æbleskiver).*

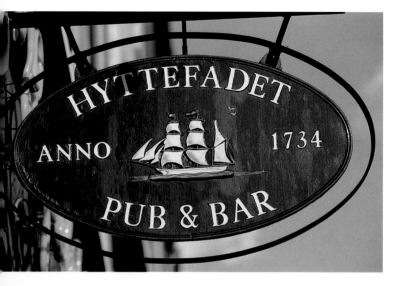

76 and 76-77  Nyhavn Canal was built in 1671 to allow trade ships to access the city. Goods could thus be unloaded closer to where they were sold, greatly stimulating trade. The docks along the canal quickly became the most crowded spots in the capital. Merchants began to build their homes along the canal, choosing the picturesque Dutch style that was popular at the time. Today, these houses contribute to the enormous charm of this fascinating area. The buildings, some of which are over 200 years old, have been restored to their original appearance, with brilliant colors under sloping red-tiled roofs. Across from them, the masts of the ships that rock lazily in the canal (most of them are now anchored and have been transformed into restaurants or houseboats) create an enchanting atmosphere that looks like something straight from a painting. The ground floors of the buildings house cafés and restaurants, indicated by quaint little signs that often have a maritime theme. These places are crowded day and night – especially in the summer, when tables are set up outside. Nyhavn has become a favorite spot for tourists as well as locals, who come to sip a beer, enjoy a coffee and have a snack.

78 Every day the queens' guards, with
their characteristic uniforms and tall
busbies, leave their barracks and cross
the city to the square in front of the
Royal Palace. The solemn, slow-paced
ceremony of the changing of the guard
is held here every day at noon.

78-79 Amalienborg, the residence of
the royal family, is composed of four
perfectly identical and symmetrical
Rococo buildings set around an
enormous square. The buildings,
constructed between 1750 and 1768,
were originally owned by several
aristocratic families. They were not
converted into the royal residence
until 1794.

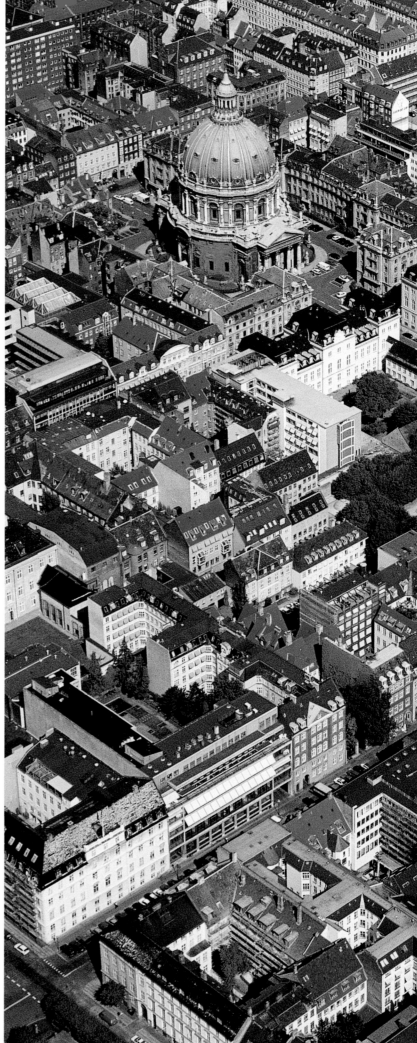

*80 top and center left  Tivoli, a favorite among Copenhageners, has recently been listed as one of the world's top 10 amusement parks. This award is a tribute to the park's mix of rides for all ages, greenery, fountains and entertainment. In fact, Tivoli is a romantic garden with flowerbeds, stunning fountains and cozy restaurants, but it also has exciting rides and attractions for children. Everyone can enjoy the mime shows, circus numbers on the enormous Plænen stage and parades of the Tivoli band and royal guards with the mini royal carriage.*

*80 center right, bottom and 81  Tivoli Park was founded in 1843. In fact, Hans Christian Andersen attended the inauguration and the park even inspired one of his fairytales. Though it has changed in appearance a number of times, it has always maintained its old-fashioned charm. It is open annually from May to September, and is one of the capital's main attractions. It becomes even more enchanting as evening falls and thousands of colorful lights turn on to outline the buildings, flowerbeds and trees. At night, the lights and fountains at Tivoli create a show within a show. Every Wednesday and Saturday the park closes at midnight with an extraordinary firework display that illuminates the sky over the capital.*

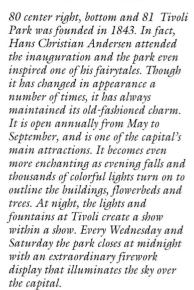

82 top  With its towers, spires and sprawling grounds, 17th-century Rosenborg Castle looks like a fairytale castle. It was built by King Christian IV, who wanted a smaller palace as his summer residence.

82 center left In the early 18th century, the Danish royal family decided to make Frederiksberg Castle its country residence because of its more convenient location. As a result, Rosenborg was used to house the crown jewels, which can now be admired in the treasury room (Skatskammer).

82 center  In 1833 the royal family decided to exhibit its collections to the public, though it retained ownership. A special museum was built to house not only the crown jewels, but also costumes, furnishings, paintings, glassware, weapons, porcelain, silver and much more.

82 center right, bottom and 83 Each room displays objects that belonged to the Danish kings and queens. The great gallery, an enormous room with a stuccowork ceiling from the 18th century, is extraordinary. There are two thrones: the "coronation throne" made of narwhal tusks and used until 1840 and a silver throne crafted in 1715. Three silver lions protect the thrones.

84-85 and 85 top left  The Ny Carlsberg Glyptotek Museum was founded in 1888 by Carl Jacobsen, owner of the Carlsberg brewery. The new museum was built so that Jacobsen's valuable collections could also be viewed by the public. Jacobsen was particularly fond of the French Impressionists, and as a result the museum has splendid paintings by Renoir, Cézanne, Monet, Degas and other artists. However, it also has masterpieces from ancient Mediterranean civilizations, such as Egyptian, Roman, Greek and Middle Eastern artifacts.

85 bottom  Thorvaldsen was inspired by the ancient world. As a result, his sculptures reflect the serene beauty that characterizes Greek and Roman works. Enthralled by classical art, he spent many years in Rome, where he made numerous sculptures that also made him famous internationally.

85 top right and center  Bertel Thorvaldsen (1770-1844) is considered the greatest Danish sculptor of all time. In his will, he bequeathed his own works and his collection of artwork to the city of Copenhagen and donated much of his fortune in order to build a museum to house this magnificent legacy. It took nearly 10 years to build the museum that would house this collection, but the sculptor did not live to see this work completed. In 1848 Thorvaldsen tomb was moved to the courtyard of "his" museum.

*86 top and 86-87  Christianshavn was originally built as a port district at the fortified northern end of the little island of Amager. There were ramparts on three sides, whereas the fourth one was protected by a wide moat. This area of the city is also being redeveloped: old buildings are being restored, the canals are being cleaned and work is being done to make it an increasingly attractive area.*

*86 center left  Our Savior's Church (Vor Frelsers Kirke) was built between 1682 and 1696. At the back of the apse is a large Baroque altar shaped like an aedicule, with a marble statue in the middle depicting Jesus in the garden of Gethsemane.*

*86 center right and bottom The tower-façade of Our Savior's Church is about 328 feet tall and was built between 1747 and 1752. It ends in a twisted spiral inspired by the Roman church of Sant'Ivo. It is circled by exterior steps that narrow as they rise to the top of the gilded sphere, crowned by a statue of Christ. From here, the view of the city and sea is breathtaking. On clear days you can see as far as the Swedish coast. The 47-bell carillon inside the tower was made in the early 20th century.*

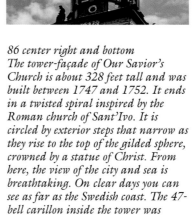

*88 top  The Gefion Fountain, in the Langelinie area, is Copenhagen's largest. Made in 1908 by sculptor Anders Bundgaard, it was inspired by the famous legend about the origin of Sjælland.*

*88 center left  Kastellet was originally a military zone set up to guard the main canal into the capital. Today it has been transformed into a park, with lovely grassy paths along what was once the rampart walk.*

*88 center right  The monumental Copenhagen Opera House was inaugurated at the beginning of 2005. It stages operas and ballets and is the only theater of its kind in Denmark, and one of the most important in Northern Europe. It faces the port canal across from the Royal Palace.*

*88 bottom  The dense network of canals and the port were once the backbone of city trade. Although they are still used for this purpose, today they are chiefly tourist attractions. Cruise ships arrive virtually in the center of town (they dock just a few yards from the Royal Palace) and guided boat tours go up and down these waterways every day.*

*89  The Little Mermaid (Den Lille Havfrue), inspired by Hans Christian Andersen's fairytale, was made by sculptor Edvard Eriksen in 1913 and was soon adopted as the symbol of the city. Every day it attracts flocks of tourists from all over the world.*

90 top and center  Despite its vicinity to Copenhagen, the village of Dragør has maintained its old-time atmosphere. In fact, 25% of its buildings – most of which date back to the 18th and 19th centuries – are protected by special laws to preserve their picturesque architecture. The port was once the haunt of fishermen and merchants – the village was originally settled by fishermen – but now it is popular above all with boaters, who stop here as they explore the coast around Copenhagen.

90 bottom  The house of author Karen Blixen, in Rungstedlund, has been converted into a museum in her memory. It has a collection of the numerous objects Karen brought back to Denmark after living in Africa. The author's African adventure inspired her famous book Out of Africa, which she wrote in this house.

90-91  The Eremitagen hunting lodge was built in the middle of the vast park of Dyrehaven during the 18th century. It is a major attraction and every day visitors cross the park in carriages, on bicycles, on horseback or on foot. Once the royal hunting lodge, it is now open to the public and has become one of the Copenhageners favorite spots for daytrips.

92-93 *The fortress of Helsingør was built in 1420 to guard the Strait of Øresund, a vital trade and military route between Denmark and Sweden. The castle was built in the second half of the 16th century but had to be reconstructed a few decades later, following a terrible fire.*

93 top *Because of its strategic position, the port of Helsingør has always been an important crossroads. Until the bridge was completed, the daily ferries linking Denmark and Sweden left from here. Although now it makes fewer runs, the ferry still operates.*

# Helsingør, the fortress on the strait

93 center The symbol of man's heroism and courage in facing the most fearsome obstacles posed by destiny and nature, the sculpture portraying Hercules battling the Hydra (the mythological monster with many heads) stands majestically at the port of Helsingør, next to a Danish flag.

93 bottom Only the chapel furnishings of Helsingør Castle were saved from the terrible fire of 1629. The enormous royal dais made of carved wood, the wooden gallery of the left aisle, the benches and the pulpit with gilded decoration, all of which date to 1582, are extraordinary.

# Roskilde, the old capital

*94 top  The cathedral of Roskilde (Domkirke) has been the memorial chapel of the Danish monarchs since 1460. Chapels have gradually been added along the aisles to hold the monarchs' tombs, representing a veritable encyclopedia of different styles and tastes.*

*94 center left  The large gilded polyptych on the altar, dating to 1560, is a Flemish work with tiles portraying scenes from the life of Christ, done in a Renaissance style.*

*94 bottom  Thousands of tourists visit the cathedral every day to see the artwork inside, but also to take a "walk through history."*

*94 center right and 94-95  The cathedral was built over the place where the Viking king Harald Bluetooth erected the city's first church in 980 (he was later buried there). At the time, Roskilde was the capital of Denmark and the church, which was later reconstructed in 1170 to make it larger and more lavish, had to reflect this role. Today it is the largest church in the country. The interior is magnificent, with a nave and two aisles divided by composite pillars. It was inscribed on UNESCO's World Heritage List in 1995.*

95

# Odense, the historic heart of Funen Island

*96-97 The historic district of Odense, the main city of Funen and one of the oldest towns in Northern Europe, has meticulously been restored to just how it was in the 18th-19th century. Its cobblestone streets are lined with half-timbered houses and small dwellings painted in pastel colors.*

*97 top and center  The Cathedral of St. Canute (Sankt Knuds Domkirke) is located near the town hall of Odense. It is named after the king-saint who was murdered nearby during a rebellion and is buried in the crypt. It was built in the late 13th century over a previous church and took three centuries to complete. The interior, finished in white plaster, is dazzling. The enormous gilded altarpiece, sculpted in 1520, is over 16 feet tall and 20 feet wide and decorated with over 300 wooden figures.*

*97 bottom left and right  The signs on shops, cafés and restaurants also commemorate Hans Christian Andersen and his fairytales. The great writer was born in Odense in 1805 and his childhood home has been transformed into a museum. His personal effects, letters and photographs are exhibited here, and there is also an extensive library of books written by and about Andersen. Fyrtøjet, the children's cultural center annexed to the building, is where youngsters can discover the world of Andersen's fairytales through fun and games.*

# Romantic Faaborg

98-99 and 99  The town of Faaborg, overlooking the sea and surrounded by woods, is one of the most romantic spots in charming Funen. Its quaint little dwellings (in the pictures) light up the historic district with their pastel colors, and there are many well-preserved half-timbered houses. One of them is Gamle Gård, a lovely house built in 1720, which has beautiful collections of porcelain, glassware, textiles, ceramics and more, bearing witness to the city's past as a trade center. Be sure to see the city museum (center right), housed in a building from the early 20th century that is considered the prototype of modern Danish Neoclassicism. Inside there is a collection of paintings by Funen artists, as well as works by sculptor Kai Nielsen.

A peaceful stroll to see the town's 18th- and 19th-century houses, which seem to huddle together, is the perfect way to experience the enchanting atmosphere of this lovely place. You feel as if you've been set down amidst dollhouses or in the middle of a naif painting; and the port (bottom right), with its boats rocking gently by the wharfs, contributes to Faaborg's fairytale atmosphere. Faaborg is set in an inlet closed off by a little island: even nature lends a hand here, adding to the charm of this magical place.

# The Viking port of Ribe

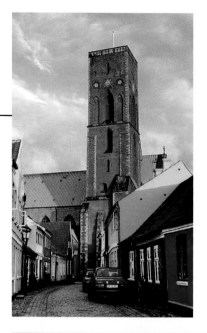

*100 center left* Ribe, the capital of the county of Ribe, is in southwest Jutland. It was founded in the 9th century AD, making it one of the oldest in the country. Its name comes from Latin: 14th-century documents refer to it as Portus Ripeis, alluding to its position on a riverbank.

*101* An aerial view gives us an idea of the winding roads here, which trace the routes of the mediaeval city. The view here takes in the river, the flat countryside and the sea.

*100 top, center right and bottom* The square tower of Borgertårnet was completed in 1333. It testifies to the second construction phase of the cathedral of Ribe, which was founded in the first half of the 12th century and was constructed in three stages. The first was the Romanesque phase, when the edifice with a nave and two aisles and the forepart with two towers (only one is still standing) on the west side were completed. During the third phase – the Late Gothic – it was enlarged to form a nave and four aisles. The church was damaged over the centuries by natural events and unfortunate restoration work, but its original appearance was reconstructed in the early 20th century. The Romanesque entrance, with the sculpture of The Deposition from the Cross, is striking. Inside, the bronze baptismal font dates from the 15th century.

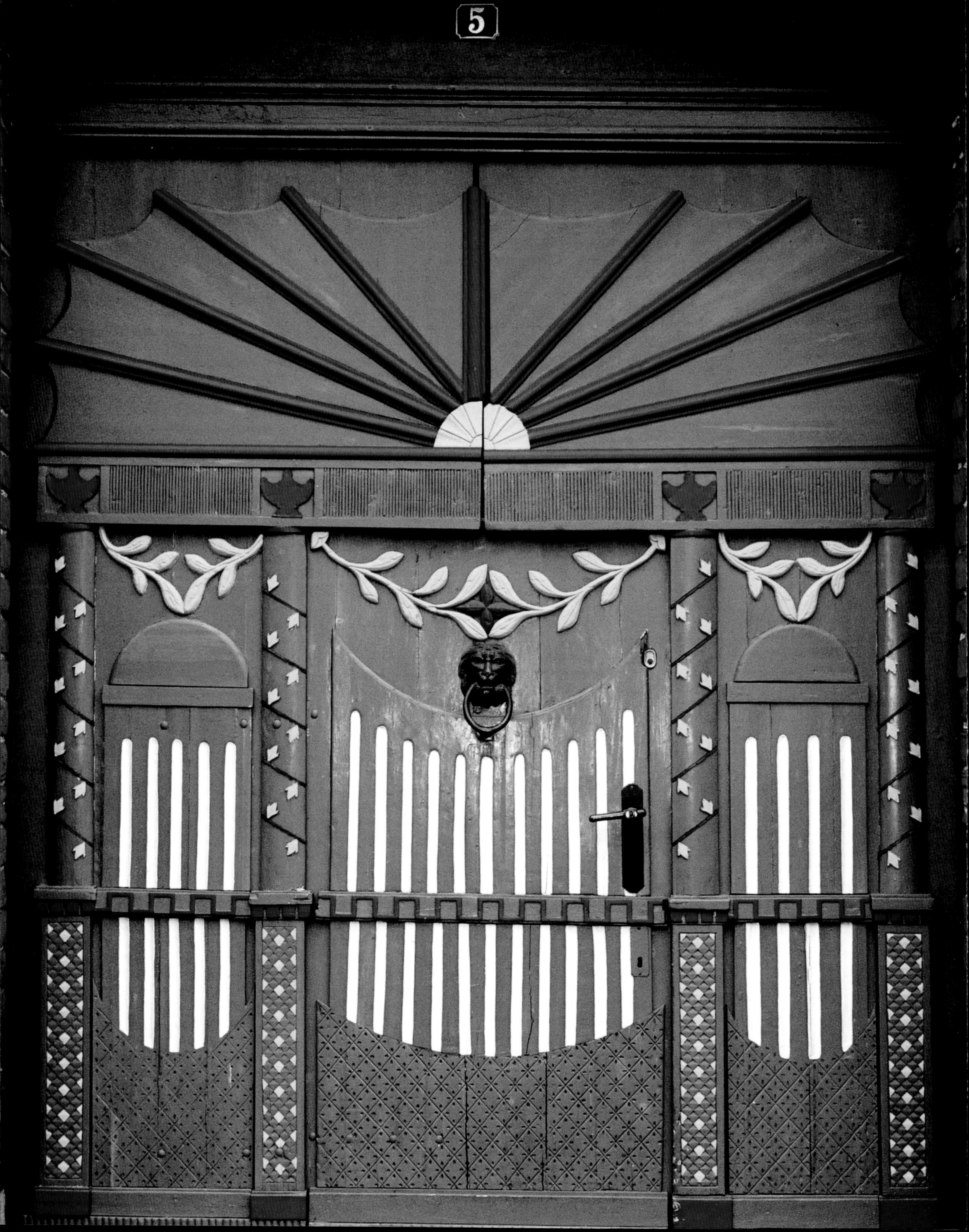
5

*102  Carved doors are characteristic of the old houses here. Some of the carvings are beautifully painted in bright colors.*

*103 top left  Over 100 buildings in the historic district of Ribe have been listed as national monuments. As a result, you can often see very old houses with the crooked walls characteristic of the Middle Ages and picturesque half-timbered structures.*

*103 top right  During the summer, the night watchman, wearing his characteristic garb, walks the streets of Ribe carrying a lantern, singing old songs, recounting old legends and beckoning passers-by to follow him on his rounds.*

*103 bottom  Even the more modern houses, with their colors and plants at the front steps, have a scenic vintage air in order to reflect Ribe's old-fashioned atmosphere. The citizens are very proud of their ancient roots, and they work hard to preserve and enhance every sign of the past.*

# Møgeltønder: southern magic

*104-105 and 105 top  Møgeltønder, in southern Jutland, is the place to go to experience the romantically authentic spirit of Danish villages. Located just a few miles away from the larger town of Tønder, Møgeltønder was built to house the staff of Schackenborg Castle, a 17th-century palace surrounded by a lovely Rococo park and now the residence of Prince Joachim, the second son of Queen Margrethe II and Prince Henrik of Denmark. Slotsgade (the road to the castle, shown in the pictures) is lined with virtually identical buildings shaded by majestic linden trees. These brick houses with thatched roofs, bow windows and decorated doors were built between the 18th and 19th century.*

*105 center and bottom  The little Romanesque-Gothic church in the village of Møgeltønder, built for the residents of the castle and their servants, was restored in 1897. Inside there are lovely Renaissance frescoes, an organ built in 1679 – the oldest one still in use in Denmark – and a carved reredos behind the altar, done in a Late Gothic style and dating from the early 16th century.*

# Århus, crossroads of modernity and tradition

*106-107 and 107 top St. Clement's Cathedral (Sankt Klemens Domkirke) is the main religious structure in Århus, the country's second-largest city and the main city of continental Denmark. The church was founded in 1201, but extensive work has been done on it over the centuries. The tall spire – which rises to a height of nearly 330 feet tall – was added in 1921.*

*107 center left The Town Hall of Århus was built between 1938 and 1942. It was designed by architects Arne Jacobsen (famous above all for his furniture design, including the Egg Chair and the Ant Chair) and Erik Møller. The building, an excellent example of Danish functionalist architecture, is topped by a 197-foot clock tower.*

*107 center right and bottom The city of Århus is known for its lively culture and social life. Countless restaurants and cafés, exhibition venues, cultural centers, shopping areas, theaters and museums offer an array of initiatives throughout the year. The Musikhuset Concert Hall, an ultramodern auditorium with glass walls (1982), stages performances by the Århus Symphony Orchestra. When the weather is nice, everything immediately moves outdoors.*

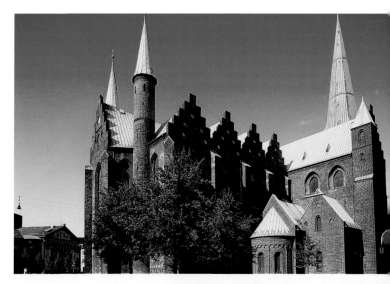

108-109 and 109 *The Old City (Den Gamle By) is a fascinating outdoor museum that offers a detailed reconstruction of daily life in a Danish town many years ago. Over 60 houses of all shapes and sizes – dating from 1570 to 1900 – have been brought in from all over Denmark and have been perfectly reconstructed. The original furnishings (or other furniture from the same period) have been set up inside. The numerous figures in period costumes enact different everyday activities, from baking bread to running shops, working as carpenters and milking cows. Small collections of handicrafts and popular artwork can be seen inside some of the houses. For example,*

*the Århus burgomaster's house (1825) has a small museum of furnishings from the 17th- to19th centuries, and the Næstved house has an 18th-century warehouse with toys and musical instruments from this period. The scenery is perfect, and visitors go from the cobblestone streets to the square (top right) and the waterway, viewing the baker's house, the mill with its enormous wooden wheel (bottom right), the church and the dairy. Thanks to the philological accuracy of the curators, who have not overlooked a single detail in this delightful reconstruction, visitors feel as if they have stepped back in time.*

# Aalborg, the dazzling queen of Limfjorden

*110-111 Jens Bang's Stone House (Jens Bang Stenhus) was built in 1624 and was the home of a wealthy merchant. It is one of the loveliest and oldest buildings in Aalborg. On the ground floor of the building, located along Østerågade, one of the city's main streets, the Svane Apotek pharmacy has been in business for over 300 years.*

*111 top The modern-looking Museum of Art (Nordjyllands Kunstmuseum) was built between 1968 and 1972 and designed by famous Finnish architect Alvar Aalto. It holds an enormous collection of works by masters such as Mirò, Max Ernst, Chagall and Picasso as well as paintings by countless Danish and Scandinavian artists. It also hosts extemporaneous shows.*

*111 center and bottom The city of Aalborg, the fourth-largest in Denmark, was built along the south bank of Limfjorden, the wide fjord that cuts across the northern end of Jutland. It is a modern and vital city with a very active port that is important to the area's industries and businesses. Its modern buildings pose a sharp contrast to the historic district, with its quaint little houses set around the Church of St. Botolph (Sankt Budolfi Kirke) and the main road of Jomfru Ane Gade, the heart of the city's nightlife.*

# The warm face of the north

*112 top  In northern countries like Denmark, people head outdoors as soon as the sun comes out. City parks are the ideal place to relax, take a break from work during the day, study or meet friends.*

*112 bottom  Viking history is a constant presence: historic reconstructions of battles or other moments in the life of this population are some of the country's most popular and widespread events.*

*113  The Danes' sociability belies the Scandinavians' reputation for coldness. For people of all ages, any occasion – even a quick snack – is a wonderful opportunity to get together.*

# In love with the great outdoors

114-115 *The field by the row of old houses is an inviting place to stop. The Danes love spending time outdoors and their cities cater to this. Even the biggest cities have extensive parks and gardens.*

115 *Motivated by environmental concerns and the desire for a healthy lifestyle, most Danes use bicycles to get around. There are bike paths along all the main streets, and there are bike racks everywhere. Professionals ride to work, painting an odd picture with their neckties flying and their jackets carefully folded and strapped to their bicycles. Handy accessories allow parents to take toddlers to nursery school and around town. Nevertheless, children learn to get around on bicycles at a very early age. An extensive network of bike trails crisscrosses the country – even in the most remote places that can't be reached by car or other motor vehicles – and this makes it easy to use bicycles to go on vacation.*

116 top and 116-117 The pedestrian areas found in every Danish city are the natural stage for street artists. A group of rambunctious young people performs an impromptu break dance in Copenhagen's historic Amagertorv, to the amusement of passers-by.

116 center There are also plenty of artists performing very demanding numbers, and tightrope walkers, fire-eaters and acrobats show off their talents. Some of the artists return to the same place day after day, attracting a regular audience.

*116 bottom  The Jazz Festival is one of Copenhagen's most interesting and popular music events. The festival is held annually at the beginning of July. In addition to concerts in auditoriums and "institutional" spaces, some of the concerts also take place in the streets, squares and pedestrian areas.*

*117  Children are particularly intrigued by the spectacle of fake statues. This one – Silverman – moves with measured gestures whenever a spectator tosses a coin in his hat.*

# Legoland, the ultimate playground

*118 top  Invented by a carpenter in 1932, Lego became one of Denmark's most important industries in a matter of decades, and it is one of the most successful toys in the world.*

*118 center  Legoland Park, not far from the Lego factory in Billund, in central Jutland, was inaugurated in 1968 and rapidly became one of Denmark's leading attractions. It is a constantly changing spectacle that appeals to the different desires of its countless enthusiasts.*

118 bottom  *Rides and attractions (many of which are made of Lego bricks) for children and adults, restaurants, cafés and shows turn a day at Legoland into an unforgettable experience – but just one day is never really enough!*

118-119  *One of Legoland's main attractions is the scale reconstruction of world cities and monuments. Some of the most fascinating recreate famous districts in Copenhagen, and there is even a reproduction of the presidents' heads sculpted at Mount Rushmore.*

*120 A giant ballerina, naturally made of Lego bricks, keeps a young visitor company during a well-deserved rest stop.*

*121 top left  For young visitors, a spin at the race track designed for little Lego cars – identical to the ones they've undoubtedly made at home – is a must. This is a real roadway complete with traffic signs, a railroad crossing and a control tower with a conductor who monitors the track and awards a mini-license to the best drivers.*

*121 top right and bottom  In addition to the large models of cities, the park also features a wide variety of theme sections, including a jungle, a pirates' area and the Far West, with gold diggers and Indians. There is also an area for toddlers, with little brick houses in which they can play. Each area has theme rides, reproductions of famous monuments, life-sized figures – the perfect photo opportunity! – and enormous containers full of Lego bricks in all shapes, colors and sizes, where visitors can have fun building something and letting their imaginations run wild. So far, 35 million bricks have been used to create the different attractions, but this number increases every year as new constructions are added.*

121

# Viking roots

*122-123 The Center of Viking Culture in Ribe (Ribe Vikingecenter) hosts Viking markets and various activities connected with the period, such as falconry displays. The nearby museum examines the history of the first outdoor market, set up in the 8th century and active for an entire millennium.*

*123 top and bottom The Viking period is also the era that, in the collective imagination, has left the biggest mark on the history of Denmark. Countless Danes trace their roots and historic memory to the bygone era when the Vikings ruled the seas. This explains why events about this population, like the Viking Festival at Århus, are so popular.*

124-125, 125 and 126-127 The Århus Viking Festival is held annually in the last week of July. "Vikings" arrive from all over Scandinavia, and entire families set up tents and participate in a picturesque market of theme objects made of wrought iron, wood, fabric, ceramics, bone and more. The highlight of this crowded international rendezvous is the staging of battles between enemy factions (on this page, left and bottom right). The Vikings wear their striking armor (this page, center) – contrary to popular belief, they did not have horns on their helmets – and challenge each other to fierce duels before an enormous audience that noisily sides with its favorites. The shows with Iceland ponies, a small but hardy breed common during the

Viking era, are also very popular (opposite page, large photograph; this page, top right), and horsemen set off at gallop on daredevil rides. These festivals are characterized by their highly accurate reconstructions of Viking settings, customs and costumes. Attention is paid to every detail, reflecting a true passion for this historical era. There are even banquets where visitors can taste typical "Viking food" as well as other areas where one can try a variety of theme activities such as archery.

*128 An enormous thermometer in City Hall Square in Copenhagen measures the temperature. At the top, a girl on a bicycle appears at the window if the weather is nice, and a figure carrying an umbrella comes out if rain is expected.*